# TO SING IN THE LANGUAGE OF BEES

Poetry and Illustrations by Gena Cohen

# Contents:

**Honey and Garden Dirt**

The music of honey
Give it to me now I beg of you
Or else I will not be able to bear the bitterness of the story
I dig my garden-dirt hands into the jar
And black fingernails bring the sweetness to my lips
Translucent nectar hits my bloodstream
Now I fly like the bees
My small wings flutter
I bury myself in the work of pollen and fragrant blooming flowers
Noble business to distract from a chest that aches with sadness
Although the weight of tragedy rests upon my back
My toes dig into the dirt
And with my spoon full of honey
I carry on.

2

**As Sun and Cloud Make Pearl in the Skies**
The drums of thunder echo against the mountain,
Then his lover lightning strikes
I am ignited by their matrimony
Like Zeus taking a match to a paper doll,
I am struck and now I crackle in flame
Surpassing flesh and bone, I am taken.
Oranges, pinks and violets I become
Flowers in the garden of Olympus
I train under the gods
Learning ascension and truth-seeing.
Teach me to infuse my words
With the cosmic grace of the pearlescent skies
Let my barks of expression turn into the sweetness of the song bird.
May my pen and page be like magic.
As sun and cloud make pearl in the skies.

**The Honey of Aquarius**
While visiting the skies,
I swallowed the moon, and all of the stars
Every planet spilled and splashed into my steaming cup of green tea and honey.
The universe tastes wild.
You see, the honey makes the world go round.
As the piano of Isis plays on,
She sings in codes of the amber nectar.
While stirring great pots of this liquid gold,
She heals the sick through music sung in the language of the bees.
The bees make homes of wax that even the sun cannot melt,
Winged warriors, armed to sting only if needed.
Prepared to die for their Queen.
The songbird sings as the winged bees hide in their blooms.
Every flower marks a birth in the animal kingdom.
Isis warns against picking the flowers.
"Don't take away their roots."
With the kiss of Isis' wings, I too fly.
I am the sun
With wings of beeswax this time these wings of mine do not melt.

6

**The Genius Creature**

Sometimes the genius needs to be coaxed out of hiding.
I leave my offering at the foot of the cave
In the form of a letter.

Dear genius creature,
If you agree to fly above me
May your wings be honored by my words.
And may your fierce heart
Be captured in virtue by the lyric of my pen.

As the piano plays,
I place blue flowers at your feet:
We fly together in the sun.

Life is one breath.
One movement of the genius creature's wings.

## The Penmaker

If every life is a line,

Then birth marks the time when the pen first touches the page.

The baby naturally grows and the pen begins to move the line forward.

And exquisitely the line of a life begins.

The pen moves in splendid twists and turns

The lines of laughter hold a light and an innocence.

The creature who lives the lifeline chooses its direction

However there is a gentle invisible hand that holds sway, and this hand belongs to the Penmaker.

**White Wildflowers Upon Black Ash**
I succumb to the momentum
I am spinning.
Suddenly I am flame.
I hiss and I lick when they come too close.
The spin had become too much to bear.
With hands over my ears, I am crouched on the floor
Glimpses of sky coax me to carry on
Even when forced to breathe in the smoke.
Acrid coughs.
Small white wildflowers bloom upon the ground of my black ash.

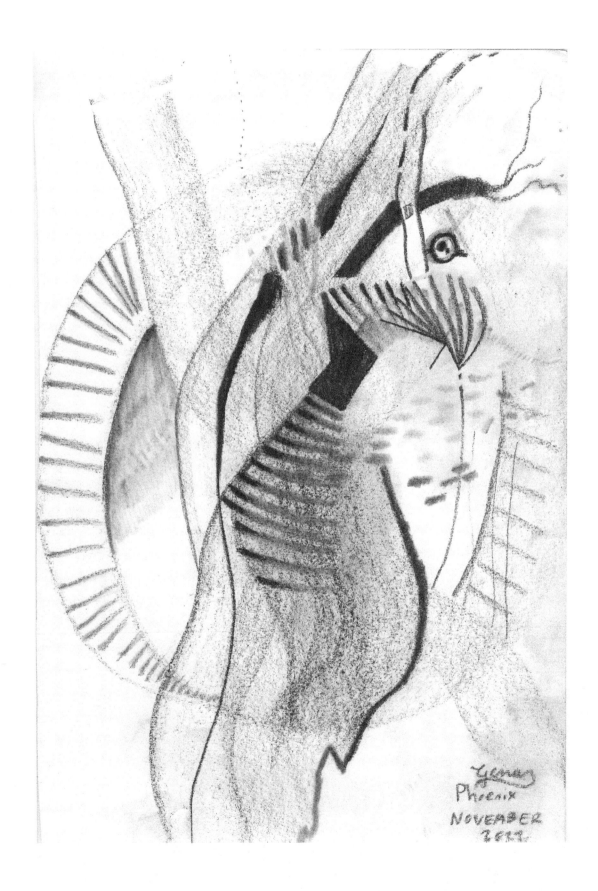

11

## Roses

You plant roses on my spine with your lips
I am immersed in hot water with you.
Drown me in your steaming cup of tea.

**At Night**
With both eyes closed,
I walk into my future,
The melody accompanies the walk.
Sometimes it's a run.
At night I am at sea with the saints and my cat on a wooden sailboat.

I have crafted this life of mine
With my two bare hands.
Knuckles, skin, and bone
All have been laid bare at one point or another.
But in that sailboat,
My hands, they heal.
Healed by healing.
Gifted by giving
Served through service.
Under blue and purple aurora borealis.

**Dark Eyes**

I take a grand bite of that orange.
It's all in the initial bite,
No matter what you're after.
Through the moonflowers of California,
I see a pair of dark eyes
That spill water for the plantlife to grow by.
There are wet-sand spots marking my knees
From when I prayed that I might become the ocean.
She brought me to the clouds on her shell shaped zephyr.
It was there that I saw her dark eyes again,
So awake.

NOVEMBER
2012

15

**To Marry the Sea**

There is mystery in the who, in the how and within the marrow of the why underneath.

Like grabbing a giant rock only to find the bottom covered in abalone shell.

But I can't marry the sea.

So do I go around again?

Around the merry-go-round of love?

There is strumming of guitar,

As I try on lifepaths in various fitting rooms, restaurants, music venues, and through kissing.

"Your smile is like a field of daisies, bright and fresh."

**For a Spin or Two**

I am looking for a kindred soul
Then there's the invisible chemistry of time.
I like to believe that the Time Master has everything planned perfectly.
The sun holds us steady as invisible passages open and close.
The clock twirls me around with you for a spin or two.

NOVEMBER 2022
Gesualdo

20

**Blood Like Ink**

With a melancholic splash
My blood is like ink in the water
Beautiful almost
Had I not stepped into the red shoes of foolishness again.
My mind runs like the wind to a past lover
And hands of longing thaw by the warmth of this old flame.

**In the Dry**
Like yellow grass in the sun,
I smoke and I burn.
Dry and hot.
The flames lick at my bare skin,
I run like a fever in the wind.

Whispers of
Wisdom

Gaia Cohen

25

**Mo(u)rning**

Morning and mourning

Words not so dissimilar as we mourn the dreams of the night past upon our waking.

**Foliage**

New grass, innocent and fresh.
The lungs of the planet are green.
I inhale their exhale
And as they exhale my inhale
I would say that we make a beautiful team.
Do you think so too?

29

**A Love Letter to my Skin**
My skin,
Supple and marred
She gets me around
She keeps me together.
Freed from anxiety in believing that my body should be different
Thank you my skin,
For housing all of me
Big and voluptuous, let me take up space in all of my beauty.
Every stretch mark,
Scars, and the lines of my hands.
The skin of my vocal chords shakes
As I scream and wail my love song.

DECEMBER 2022
Gerald

31

**Pink Balloon**

The guitar plays in the cafe
I catch your eye.
Anxiety isn't welcome but I see it in your eyes.
Here I am.
Trying to house a safe space for you to breathe and to feel.
I hand you a pink balloon.
It's your anxiety.
Just give it to the sky and she'll know what to do.
Liberate yourself as the knots from your gut float away with the balloon
Doesn't that feel better?
You're free now.

MOON    2022
Gena Cohen

**33**

**Bloom, Bloom, and Bloom**
The echo of wings resounds inside my chest,
A purple flower blooms by the light of the moon.
Oh Goddess, take me by the hand.

She leads me to the springs
Once arrived, I am drunk off of the nectar.
Aurora Borealis dances above
The moon sings an ethereal tune.
I dance below
One with the sky, I look him right in the eye.
We bloom, bloom, and bloom under the light of a full moon.
A dragonfly kisses my forehead.
She whispers secrets into my ears
I am safe in my velvet skin under the velvet sky.

**The Steps of Time**

As I climb the steps of Time, my view keeps changing. Sometimes things that once hurt don't hurt so much as I get higher up.

**Destined For Nowhere?**

So out of breath,

I run to you,

Hardly anything has taken place yet,

You hardly know me.

I was told everything that is to come with you.

Surely I am not being played for a fool.

I have played many parts upon this planet

And some of them have been foolish.

Do I dance to imaginary music?

Whether that be so, I dance myself into a frenzy of anticipation. Heart laid bare.

So out of breath.

My mother yells "Be! Just be in presence!" I always drive her mad with fear when I floor the gas pedal.

At least I know something is coming

One is never destined for nowhere.

With or without you...

I am not destined for nowhere.

**My Warm Drink**
Like warm drink sliding down my throat,
You slid into my life,
And I feel fond of you.
I grab at you like a cup of warm coffee
I want to devour you,
And run into the experience of my being yours
...and your being mine.
But like solid earth,
You force me to pace myself and to face myself.
I wait for tomorrow to read the next chapter,
When all that I want is to know you now
To touch you and to read all of you tonight.
With skin like soft velvet
And with eyes like the Lake from which you were born.
Will this be a true love story, I ask you?
For I have been talking to the Fates.
Time is relishing in my torture,
Forcing me to work with the gods of patience
For there exists a flame that longs to live fiercely and freely now.
And I have been told that it is you who I am to love.

**A Beauty Beyond the Sun**
Beyond the light of the sun what is there?
The light of the Great Sun is everything to us.
If she were to die, we would all go with her.
I am devoted to her as she shines
She is turning the grass under my feet green as I write.
Particularly how she has coupled with water has left me like a child who has seen the most beautiful thing.

**Or Would I Break with the Beauty of it**
Dare I ask what lies beyond the sun?
For she is the very breath within my lungs.
Beyond her, is there some form of a higher love?
Perhaps there is a word for something stronger than anything I have ever known.
Something completely foreign to us in her illumination.
Beyond the light of the sun
Could I even take this in?
Or would I break with the beauty of it...

44

## Moved

As we may gaze at the unknown with skepticism and with the sight of the cynic,
I cannot help but place spectacles of wonder over my eyes.
To be in search of something so saturated beyond the illumination of love
That there is an element within me that melts
And all that is left are the tears of a woman who is deeply moved by a part of existence
So fresh, so innocent
That is the beauty of living by which that is beyond the sun.

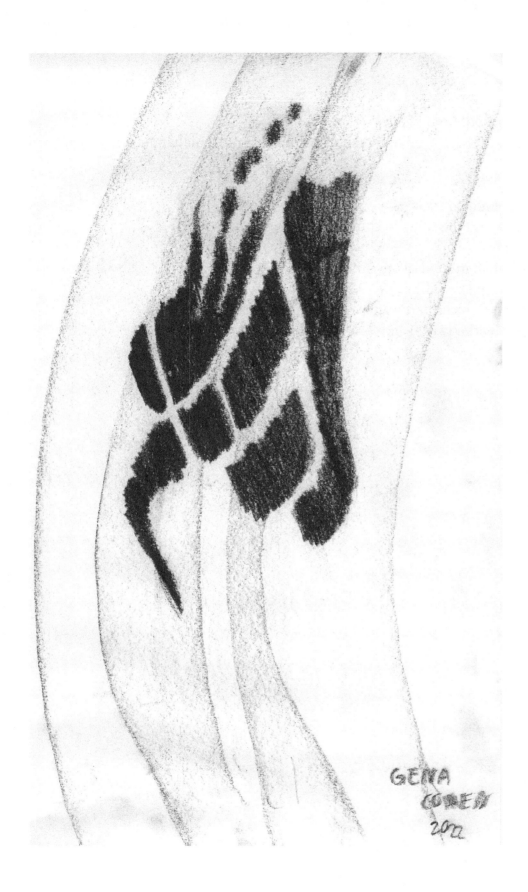

46

**I am Rock**

As I gaze into my eyes in the mirror
I see assurance where I did not before.
I see acceptance where there used to live the fearful beast of Denial and his partner Shame.

Here I am today, like naked rock
Shaped by the winds and the rains to stand as I am.
Unabashed and honest.
May the future behold a myriad of beautiful presence.
There are violet and white wildflowers
That grow within the crevices and cracks of my hard surfaces.
Rugged and shaped by the various forces of the elements

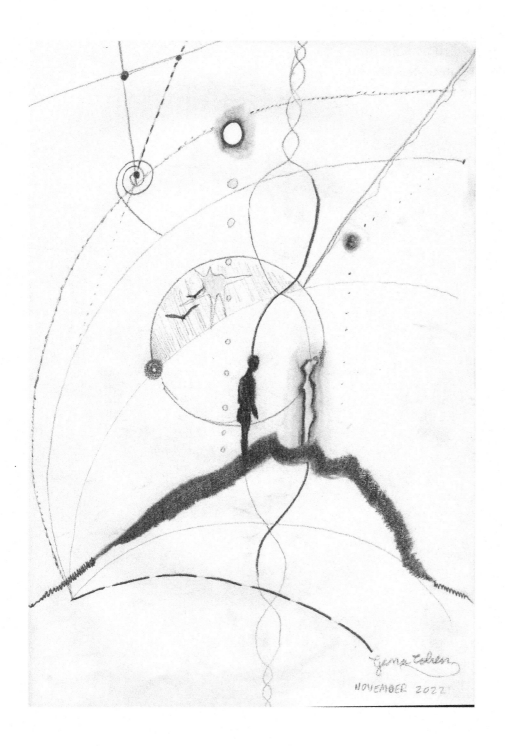

NOVEMBER 2022

48

**Hey River**

Hey river, yeah river
Why did you let this happen to me?
What a fracture, what a break.
I couldn't see the sun in your water for so long.
There was a great storm.
You, river, you're supposed to protect me.
With light in your eyes, I come back to you
The water of the river, the water of a mother.

NOVEMBER
2022
Gene Tolu

**Onward**

I carry onward
What's left of me?
What's left of the one in mania?
The girl with one foot in euphoria and the other in a hell
Is safe now.
Safety like warm bread from the local bakery in a house by the lake.
I cry out as I stare at my eyes reflecting back in the lake water
Family has planted me in the soil once again.
Wildflowers are scattered today in the yard.
My head is out of the skies and my feet back to ground.
Onward.

52

**Soon They Will Bloom**

The flowers of yesterday were picked,
And today there are new seeds that rest under the blanket of snow.
Soon they will bloom

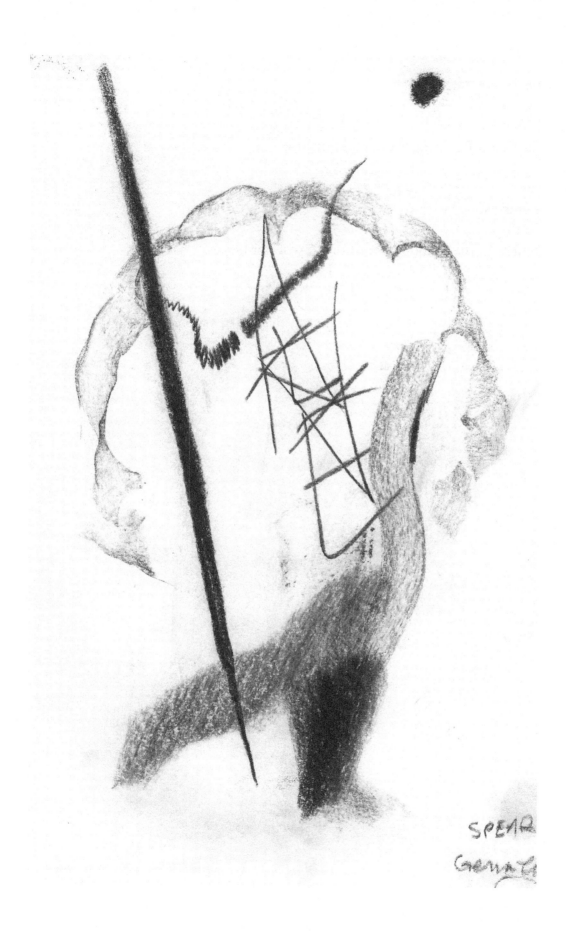

SPEAR

George

54

**Mollie**
She is something beautiful,
Flawed perhaps,
But her heart brims full of light
Racing to find an ecstatic joy, meaning and purpose,
She runs wild:
Breath heavy.
Light igniting her eyes,
She knows no limit
At night, she returns to the cocoon of comfort to rest her bones.
Anam Cara.

**Windfall**

Peace like a river, peace like the sea,
Whoa! She jumped right off that cliff and into the salt water.
Only a splash of white remained as the ocean swallowed her up.
What did she feel as she fell?
What did she see under the ice water?
With eyes reborn.
Did all of her troubles fly off of her as she fell?
Gone with the wind of the fall?
She popped right back up, like a buoy.
She laughed beautifully alive, as her wet self
Returned to land, unscathed.
Warm breath paints the icy air.
Alive and with a wildness still coursing through her blood.

**The Bare Naked Truth**
There is a synthesis
At the cracking of the glass of illusion
I laugh
As it's a great borrowing,
We shall keep nothing when we pass.

58

**The Wounded Deer**

The wounded deer,
Is not forsaken to a life of pain.
Perhaps her very wound,
This wound that she has worn for the first half of her life, bleeds blue.
For somewhere along the way
She began to understand
That this pain was a portal to understanding some greater truth.
The prayer beads collide.
Even as her wound bleeds,
She leaps high and she tastes the life of her survival.

NOVEMBER
2012

60

**Snow Flower**

Wildflowers scattered upon snow
While gazing at the sun,
I am full of light
I am a diamond in the snow amidst a field of wildflowers.

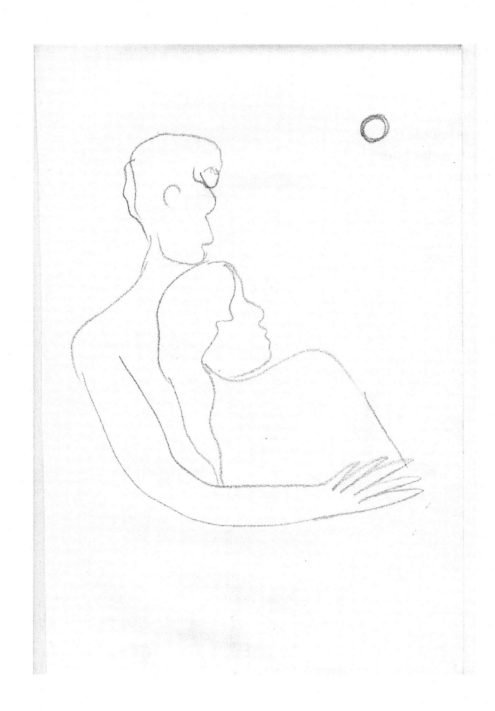

65

**Warm Water**

Warm water,
The lyrical song of rain dancing on skin.
Breath fogging windows
After jumping into a car with you.
Warm bodies, steaming air.
The rain drums on the hood of the car
As your lips explore my left collar bone.
Daisies bloom in the spring.
The sting of the bloom
The beauty of it almost hurts.

64

**Melted Hearts**

She played coy,

Slipping and sliding from his grasp.

Destiny cannot be evaded however

It is inevitability.

Two hearts collided and the dynamo of hearts exploded into great shining of orange flame

"Good" he spoke while smiling into her elusive eyes.

Now with a heart like warm wax, there was a fusion of something new and fresh called love

"Good," she smiled back.

**Stubborn Hope**

Let Hope reverberate in your very bones
No matter how hard you may fight her,
May she root down stubbornly,
Like the tree that won't fall, oh grandmother.
When you want it to end,
May she shake the very existence that beats the blood from your heart.
And we'll sing her song together.
Stubborn hope.
She's beautifully stubborn, that one she is.
May hope live as an iron chain that won't break.

**Under the Light of the Moon**

Peace like a river, peace like the sea.
I am emerged into the ancient salt waters
Fluid, wild and liberated into the depths
I grow gills and a shimmering tail
Shells gather in my long hair and cover my naked chest.
The sea I become.
I am a mermaid.
It's safe in the water,
I ask the two legged women who walk on land
Do you see me, as I see you?
The rhythms of the waves crash in a lull
And cradle me to sleep under the light of the moon and by the salt of the sea.

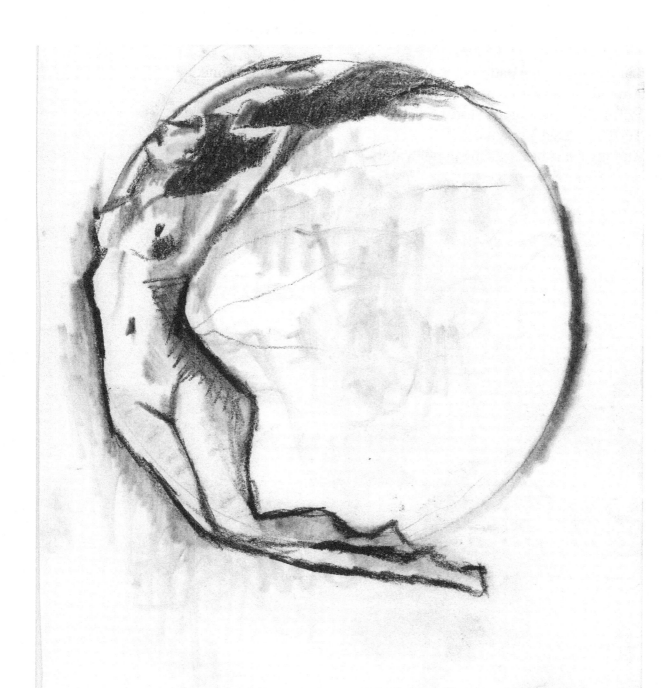

NOVEMBER
2022

### The Great Lake Remains - Gitchi-Gami - Lake Superior

As sun and water make magic
This experience of paddling in the lake of diamonds is a holy one.
After all of those who have come and gone
Within the pages of my story,
The Great Lake remains,
And my heart beats strong in her waters.

72

## The Mother Bird

She enveloped me in her golden wings
Only the light of the sun
And the love of the mother bird
Was allowed in this shrine
There was no cold allowed in here

74

**Pearl**

One day these bones that carry me through
Will become grains of sand.
Maybe the ribs that encase my heart
Once I'm long gone and turned to dust
May become pearls in the oysters.
For every Pearl begins as a grain of sand
Before the oyster transforms her.

**Red Bloom**
Like a red flower bursting through virgin snow
The power of the bloom trembles the clay of the earth.
The beauty quakes the knees of even those upon the steadiest of ground.

**In My Cup of Tea**
I drink in the blue sky.
The great water bearer pours the atmosphere down my throat until I am nearly full.
All of life inside of me
Around the sun, the planets orbit inside my belly.
I can feel it all.
Every birth.
Every suffering.

The bird's broken wing mends.
The child survives the car crash.
The grandfather passes on.
The seed becomes sapling
The sapling becomes tree.
The moose says goodbye to her young in a rage.
The baby's first word is love.
Time etches skin.

I breathe, and with a hiccup,
I return to Self.
To Gena
I am Gena again.
I am also infinity in a spilled drop of tea.

December
2022

## Candle

I light a candle for every moment of wholeness and light in my life, and I place my left hand on the shoulder of the woman who suffered. Every moment that she suffers I go to her in time and place my hand upon her shoulder, and may she know that she is not alone.

NOVEMBER
2022
Gina Lin

82

**She Paints**
Dear breath that fills my pink lungs,
Am I a character of tragic circumstance?
Life, so full of grace...
I cling to my paints.
The pen and page too
The saints watch over me by the light of the moon.
I have to create with all that is within me.
I never could have guessed that there would be torture in my life.
In my two hands, I hold two stones, a dark and a light one.
When all reason is gone, it is beauty and the naked truth that I guard close to my heart.
May the candle be lit.

"No, It's not simply tragedy. It's an epic." She whispers gently.

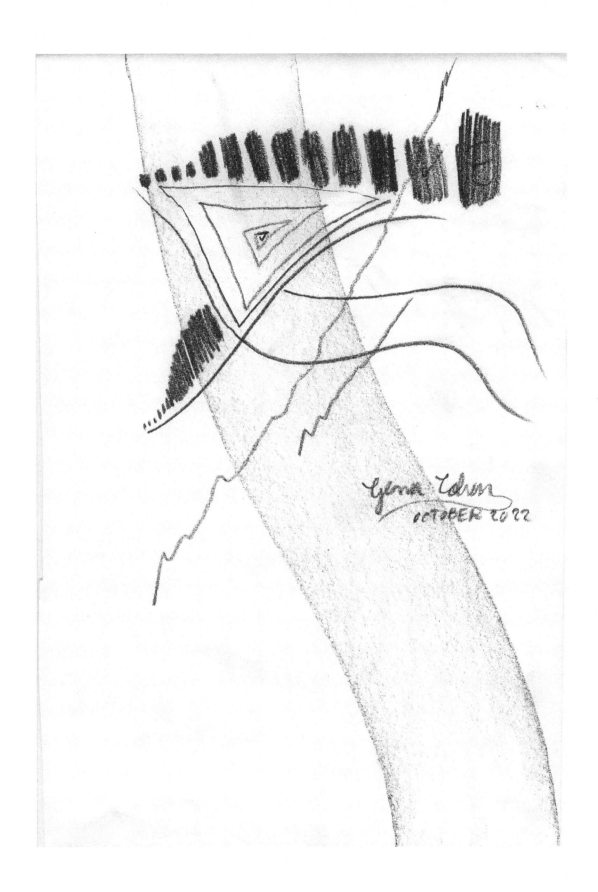

**Ra**
The sun guards me by day
I orbit around her.
She gives me golden light to live by.

**The Euphoria of Belonging**
In the night, the moon pulls my spirit into the land of dreams.
With eyes closed in the body's rest,
My chest rises and then falls in breath.
Like the waves of the ocean, crest and crash.

The night speaks in silver light. Lunar.
"Tell me if you love me," I hear my voice whisper in a dream.
I am speaking to my own reflection.
So I look at this woman's crying eyes.
Finally they are honest.
I am baptized in the salt water.
I feel the illuminated force of kinship with the water of the pearls.
The moon cradles me in the gentle euphoria of belonging.

November
2022

**Blue Beads**

With blue beads around my neck that were once a rosary, I have some words to say.
"To the one behind the curtain,
You are really something.
You have been nurturing me back to wholeness and this hand of yours upon my shoulder
Brings me comfort like the rays of the sun on skin."

"I will take care of you." You speak with only a smile


I place a pink rose at your feet
As you teach me how to use my wings.

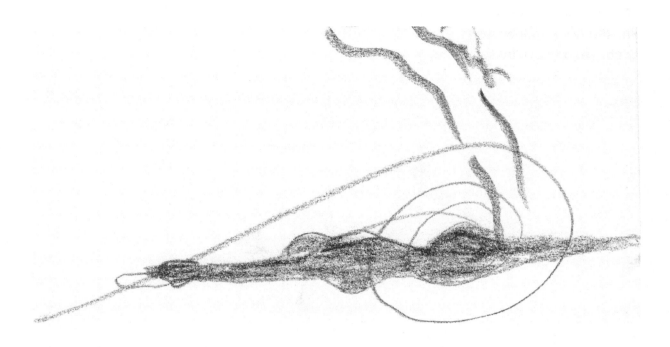

90

## The Mercy of the Sea

Fall on my knees,
I have the ocean's soul,
She did not swallow me
Even when I gave myself to her.

Lynn Cohen
October 2022

**The Bow**
My story is my own for what it is worth.
I would never trade it in, not for anything.

The sun has continued to rise and set even when tragedy has hit.
And it has been these very tragedies that have taught me to bow to my humanity.

Sometimes a heart is broken open so as to allow in more light.

NOVEMBER
2022
George Cobum

94

**In the Skies**
Let her fly in the skies
To the music of the wind's howl
And if she becomes lost up in the clouds
Know that she will return
She always does.

OCTOBER 2022

**Butterfly**
Swept up by the hurricane,
Now my feet are planted on the ground again.
Quickly these roots took to the soil this time
I am nurtured with water and sun
Blooming, reaching, feeling and living.
As the butterfly perches upon my branch,
She whispers gently
"I will protect you,"
As the sun catches the blue stained glass of her wings
She flies out of sight
Carrying on with her journey
I still feel her existing out there though
Protecting me.

98

**Peace like a River**

Peace like a river, peace like the sea
We live upon a globe or water, metal and earthen substance.
Our lungs breathe in the winds that blow about the creatures we know as trees.
We rest our spines upon their trunks.

Peace like a river, peace like the sea
I swim in the great salt water.
Before my eyes would cry with the whales
People were not caring for the planet.
Seas were rising
Then a little bird named Hope joined us
She flies golden, bright and pure
And we know now that everything is going to be okay.
She flies no matter what,
A vital creature.

Peace like a river, peace like the sea
I have returned to safe waters
I can stand without being thrown to the wolves these days.
Hands of healing guided me back.
To call upon hands of healing
For the illumination upon those with troubles.

**Made from Clay**

I am a block of clay
Earthen and malleable.
As for the tender hands that shape me
Make me beautiful
For my longing
Is to discover a wholeness
Nurtured by the rainbow rays of the sun.
For my yearning is to move through this life with an ease
By the milky light of the moon, to dance without encumbrance.

As I am sculpted forth from the clay of my substance
May these precious wings of the sculpture that is my life
Find full dignity in their expression.

As the bell rings,
There is a silence.
The clay whispers its yearning "become, become."

Gena Cohon
OKTOBER
2022

## Wildflowers

Peace like a river, peace like the sea
May that which weighs heavily upon one's back be released in the meadows.
And may wildflowers grow amidst the troubles.
And along with the gentle winds
That which was once gruesome and frightful,
By water, soil and sun,
agrees to be beautiful.

103

**Safe**

Soon after I left,
White snow came from the skies and laid the ground to rest.
Do you know how we as humans can only see a fraction of the light spectrum in existence?
Well the same is true for sound I think.

One day, as I sat in a cozy chair,
With her healing hands upon my head
I took a sip of tea. Yunnan black.
The steam danced a ballet above the cup.
The taste of the tea seemed to awaken a sound that I had never heard before in my experience of living.
A chime so high, about six inches above my head to the right rang.
Soft innocence, fresh light.

My grandmother hugged me and said "I am glad that you are safe."
There's nothing quite like seeing a bird, who once had a broken wing, fly in the skies again.

105

**Love and the Bitter Drink**

As you enter into the cafe,
I want to sink into my cup of coffee.
Warm brown drink over all of my bare body
I am naked and exposed in my desire for warm bones.
For I have been corrupted by the fingers of an impossible love
Thereby leaving me no choice but to dive to the bottom of my drink
And that way you will not see
How my cheeks blush
When I hear the sound of your name.
That way you will not know
Of the nature of my blossoming daydreams
Surrounding a life with you.
The coffee has notes of cocoa and fruit
As my feet tread the dark water,
I wish to trade the bitter drink with the sweetness of your kiss.
However I will burn with that hot cup of coffee
Before you become awakened to the fact
That I am in love with you.
I build a castle with the grounds at the bottom of the glass
For you are with another.
And so I melt in my drink as I am stung by forbidden longing.

**To Cultivate my Garden**
I gather all of my flaws and every last mistake,
like a bouquet of wildflowers
Their stems full of thorns.
I nic my fingers on these rugged green spikes
To sit in my own existence,
And only I have ever and will ever get to sit in this particular existence,
It's like a laugh! The beautiful absurdity is so sweet and lovely of breathing and living.
Oh choices, how I have mulled you over.
Like a button bursting off of a coat, the pressure is released,
And gloriously even no choice made is a choice made he said.
Gloriously I beam, as I am alive.
There have been those victory blooms too that live in the garden of the last twenty six years
I continue to cultivate the garden...
Organic, and fresh, yes that's *my* garden.

**Longing and Affection**

Do you know when you eat something with a lot of spice, and the heat lingers as a burn on the inside of your lips?

Well the thought of you haunts me like this taste.

The hunger to kiss you lingers on my lips, and every nerve is enlivened.

The inside of my mouth burns with heat as the thought of you dances in my psyche,

Filled with longing and affection

**Goliath**

At the end of the fight,

My knees sink into the fragrant mud

I rest my trembling forehead on the white clay of the earth and bring my lips to the ground.

In precious acknowledgement of the mania that has become my Goliath.

I lay the hospital papers upon the altar

Every paragraph of the story lives as if upon a thin sheet of ice

I nurture the sheets into one cold thick crust

Strong enough for me to put weight on again.

As the gates of the beast's mouth open for my release

I walk back to my sanity.

**Melodies of the Moon**
Burn me down, and I resurrect like a phoenix from the ash
Shut me out, and I am the white bloom of the avalanche
crashing through the door
Drown me out at sea,
Then watch me grow gills
For I am mermaid.
After you bury me in the sand,
Step back as I melt this very sand with the flame of my conviction.
The sorrows of the wounded hearts
only exasperate
As whiskey splashes from glass to throat.
May my life be as a love letter to God
Melodies of the moon.
Like the wolves,
I howl.

**Seasons**

Immerse me in gratitude,
Let me remember that there are seasons in my own life
Just as there are seasons in the natural world.
Pour creative inspiration down my throat like medicine.
And watch me translate the unspeakable codes into my art.
I live for those unspeakable feelings
Sometimes they are flashes of light.
A carved piece of wood,
The grazing of two different peoples' skin.
A cup of tea.
To catch the light in a stranger's eyes and find them beautiful.
Even that pull of desire for someone who isn't exactly your lover... right now anyway
The heart beats like a drum,
And I'd kiss you easily.
If I could just kiss you...
Then I could finally melt and return to the sun.
You could play the guitar as I transform.
Do you know how beautiful I actually find you?
Because I do.
Find you beautiful that is.
And I want to kiss you.
You blind me of the world's destructions by your light.

**Storms**
For I live in a land that has been hit by storms.
And this has left the days where the sun is exposed feeling precious.
Today the sun shines, and the chaos of the storm has parted.
After the clouds parted, one person is left clearly visible in my heart.

**Meant to be Sung**

She dreamt of making music,
She would open her mouth, and out would crash entire oceans of sounds.
Cacophony, serenity it's all in there, in her voice
To sing the song that longed for expression in her bones,
She could feel it trapped in her throat,
Testing potentials and waiting to wail.
An aching longing

**Blue-Green Eyes**

I noticed that your eyes are a blue- green the last time we met.

Safe in the cocoon of the thought of you.

Maybe one day it will be the cocoon of your arms again.

For the light you carry, I thank you.

Because when you shine it onto me, I am stronger.

Creaky, I open to you like a bloom in the sun.

Even when I cry, your hand is on my shoulder, and I am safe by your warmth.

I want to drink your kiss.

The three words...

Will we ever be together again?

You live inside my chest.

**Metal**

Drown me in beauty
And hammer my metal
Into a great statue.

I am a statue of flesh and blood.
What this even means is something beyond what I know tangibly.
My humanity, our humanity.
Life coursing through our veins.
This life is like a great walk to find a clean mirror

## Birds in the Wind

I want everyone and everything that has ever meant something beautiful to me to stay with me, but alas that isn't the nature of living. I cannot hoard that which I love, and instead I set everyone free like birds in the wind.

## Ballads

Peace like a river, peace like the sea,
The piano plays softly
May I never get used to these sounds
Thereby may I never take them for granted.
May every harmonious note
Touch the part of me that is awe stricken
Like dropping a stone into water,
There is a ripple in the liquid.
As various ballads ripple,
Peace through my own body in sound.

**His Name was Poem**
I begin walking when a shadowed figure stops me in my tracks.
The wind floats whispers of footsteps in the hallows
With a dark hand upon my left collar bone, the veiled man does not let me pass.
Then he shares that his name is Poem,
I would have to write him in order to make sense of things...in order to carry on

So I kneel on the dirt ground, and I search his feet.
I find heartbreak in the way they meet the ground
Then I gaze at his knees. They hold the fear of past enslavement.
His hips reveal the physical labor of building something great, a cabin in the wilderness perhaps.
His shoulders, sturdy and full, reveal the pain of bearing the weight of the world for a lifetime.
Then his gray eyes... shards of pain in them along with great bursts of light. The contrast of existing, I guess.

And so I begin to write him.
His story poured out of my hands, into the ink of my pen, to be immortalized on the page.
Stories from thousands of years ago to live on through ink on rock, on parchment.
Discovered buried in the dirt along with the roots of the wildflowers.

## Pained Dirt

Plant seeds in the fragrance of pained dirt,
And never forget that every bloom naturally has to fight
To breach the dark mass of soil
I emerge victorious in the sunlight
After the noble work of sprouting roots.
Let water, sun and sumptuous minerals nourish me into full bloom.
My existence, if she may be short then let her be sweet,
For soon I am buried by the snowfall.
Composted. Real. Honest, and mortal.
Ah yes, may I live as an honest bloom,
Like the calla lily.
Like the daffodil, the flower of laughter, may I bloom, bloom, bloom
May I make music with the wind
And seed the ground with more of me
Before winter takes me back to the underground.

**A Gift from the Dreamland**
Rapture
I wrote a poem in my sleep last night
Then the stars blinked me awake so I could write it
I fear only fear itself

**Where Breathing is Easy**
To seek the pure waters
Of a life. For a life. With a life.
Is to discover that sweet spot.
Where breathing is easy

My chest is cracked open and in between the two halves of my ribcage, there blooms a flower.

The concept of commemorating pain is the white lily. A flower to mark resiliency.

Like a child who is learning to walk, I begin with fresh feet, unaccustomed to planting roots on the Earth. Then, as time passes, great wooden ropes of root expand from my feet.
I am ground, and I am red earthen clay.
Water and flame, I am.
Root and branch
Earth and sky.

**Indigo seas**
Weaver of worlds
Will you whisper to me
The gentle secrets of the earth?
What is the truth of the light?
And what lies in the mystery of the shadows?
The merging of mathematics and mysticism.
A perfect prism,
Filtering rainbow light.
An epiphany during meditation
As time moves,
This woven existence
Carries me on indigo seas

**A Book too Tall**

I realized that
I don't know the feeling
Of true belonging.
Like a book too tall
On the shelf
Amidst a series
Of perfectly color-coordinated novels of exactly the same height.
I am a poetry book amidst algebra textbooks.
I am perhaps not always steeped in sense,
But when my heart yells for me to escape,
I always find a way out.
And when this same heart beats true with somebody or something,
Well, I fall in love.

**The Peaceful Beast**
Today there are no words.
Just a silent stillness and light
That I feel shining behind my closed eyelids
As I meditate
Is peace a beast?
If so, I welcome him
Into my home.
Bring your soothing winds into my four walls.
To be inspired
But to be not thinking about anything in particular
My desires float away like dandelion seeds
As my arms open wide to hug the beast of Peace.

**Music**
The softness of the melody
Like the gentlest warm wind
That caresses the skin of my cheek.
Like the softest strumming of the guitar.
For beloved daughter
Have you ever heard a song so beautiful that
It stops everything in you?
And something in my belly quakes as all hard shell dissolves by the beauty of the music.

## Cycling

I am a windmill,
Up, down
Then cycling one thousand times over again.
I am a spoke on the wheel of your bike.
I love faster and faster.
Impossible to see
Yet a part of the greater system.
Like a grain of sand
On a soft white expanse of beach.
Struck by lightning,
I turn to glass.
In just one instant I am sea glass.
Water for the parched.
This heart of mine
Cannot help but to love you.
You are in my heart,
You are in the very pores of my skin,
The catch between my breath
The visible exhale on a cold winter day.
Yet somehow like a shaky foot on too thin ice,
We splintered,
And we were lost to the cold.

**River**

Life moves along.
Future becomes present
And present becomes past
Moments are like water
That moves through my fingertips
Impossible to hold onto
I am carved by this water.
I am driftwood.
Meandering along the river that holds my beginning and my end.
I stare into the sun.
I am one thousand suns refracting light on one thousand rivers
Love is in my blood
Musing perches on my mind
Like a butterfly
Whispers float off of her wings
"Where do I go after I die?"
I feel a truth beyond me somewhere, somehow
An eternal knowing that I shall carry on.
Perhaps finding new rivers to explore
Gathering loves along the way.

**Abalone**

The abalone shell washes up on the seashore.
Greens, blues and purples
Illumine by the light of the moon.
One million splinters of a broken moon
Glitter upon the indigo black of the ocean
Yet there she lives,
Still up in the sky, whole.
She is a full moon tonight.
Just as sometimes we may all splinter and break,
There is always a higher part of ourselves above,
Shining; whole.

**Story Books**
I bury myself in the stories inside of my books.
True comfort.
Deliciously, I devour every page.
I am taken on adventures and brought into new worlds.
Transported by small black symbols we call letters.
Sacred codes.
Words;
Love and loss inside every story.
These stories satiate something deep inside of me.

**Saltwater**
Do you roll with the waves?
These waves that have carved two faces upon me
The wise woman and the fool
One steeped in madness.
I am trying to live without harming
With paint on my hands instead of blood

Do you read my palms like a book?
As you press them into your heart.
I feel a cosmic heartbeat behind your body's clay.

I beseech you
To make every golden wish
Upon every flower's bloom
For transience is a bird
Who flies in these skies.

**Green Loves Red- Their Love Story**
The brush swirls in the red paint that rests on the glass palette
"Your painting needs some red," the master bellowed.
"A ground"
"Passion"
"Like blood, yes your painting needs to show its life force."
"Now some green, like grass, yes."
So I splash some green oil on top of the red paint on the canvas.
If the color red had a lover, who could fill these shoes but green?
Together they maintain a balance.
Green like a fresh breath, steeped in peace. Red, raw, bloodied and powerful. I continue
to paint their love story on my canvas.

## The Run - True North

How many acres must I run?
And what do I run for?
How do you feel when you run upon expanse after expanse, day after day?

Some's ankles become strong,
Their entire legs and bodies day by day
become more and more chiseled,
as god-like as Michelangelo's David.
The work is good for them.
Nourishment for the spirit.
And after the full day's run, they sleep in peace.
Hearts beautifully disciplined
And the inner compass beautifully tells them "Yes, you are on course."

Then there are others who look at the miles of green grass that is the day's run,
And hearts swell with anxiety,
It is that needle of the compass perhaps
That whispers,
"This is not your North."
And as the whistleblower yells to run, it is these characters who may stumble.
For it is only the fish who belong in the sea,
It is just the creatures of the snow who are built to withstand the cold,
Not everyone's compass points to the same direction.

**Little Things**
The window is slightly open
Warm summer air, tinged with a bit of the night's coolness wafts in.
The outdoors smell wet like fresh rain.
I sit at a worn wooden desk, the kind with marks of character.
On the second floor.
My view is of the water, a great expanse of silver ripples.
I am writing a poem, and the flickering flame dances light on my page.

To build a life that satisfies one's heart's desires,
Well isn't that the eternal question?
I pray that this question resolves in my own life, and in yours too.

**A Wet Misty Day**
As I breathe and gaze at the lake
Through the library window,
I feel everything.
It is a lot.
So I put in my music
And I listen to some classical
As the skies cry in rain.
She, the sky comforts me.
As I comfort her.
We both cry
Because we both feel it all

**Mistakes and the Sun**

When I make mistakes,
I fly to the sun
She burns away my shame.
And all is well once again.

**Wind and Sun**

That bitterness,
Take it from me,
And let me run oh so wild.
The singing winds whip my hair
And I am one with the wind and sun

**Dusk and Dawn**

As one corner of the Earth
Awakens by the light of Dawn,
Across the miles of rugged terrain
People rest their heads in darkness,
Ready for sleep.
Dawn, a Goddess who blesses us
With morning light and tangerine skies,
Is a morning wanderer.
Dusk, her twin brother
Adorns himself in soft blue and lilac blankets of sky
Explores the mystery that is night.
Together, they have choreographed their earthly dance to perfection.
The curtain of night sky and stars
Opened by the sister Dawn come morning
And gently closed by the brother Dusk come nightfall.
As I walk through the prairies throughout the day,
May I know the comfort of the friend's hand upon my shoulder as we orbit the sun on
this humble planet.
Everybody needs someone.
Like Dusk and Dawn.

**A Creaky Craggly Love Poem Written in Spring**
Take me as I am,
I may be splintered and cracked at parts,
A little broken hearted sometimes
But when the wind whispers comfort through the trees
At the advent of spring,
I find my little sliver of peace.
If I can feel the sun, *really feel her,* that's enough.
I am but a simple human
Who writes love poems in her journal.

**Cadmium Red**

I am the paint in the tube,
Squeeze me onto the palette,
And spread me generously onto the canvas;
Cadmium red and Indian yellow;
I am the marrow of every color
What is it that you will paint with me?
I am tool, yet I am subject.
Sunrise and sunset.
Like soft pink and marmalade orange.
I will bask in that sun's light
When her rays caress my paint.
Brushes thick and thin, pointed and squared dip into me.
I am your stroke of good luck.
I blow on your dice before they roll on the green felt.
I am the strike of magnesium flint and steel.
I spark and glitter with the stirred passions of the strike.
The strike of lightning; the movement of a culture.
Suddenly I can feel a place in my chest that I did not know existed before when I look at
the painting that the Artist made with me.
The crow of the rooster at dawn.
She rests her head on the softness of the pillow.
Sweet comfort, like milk and honey.
The grand kaleidoscope spins as life moves,
And the wind makes the trees breathe.
Angry hands find relief as a tight grip loosens.
The sigh of cold water on hot skin.
Cadmium red finds a music.
One trillion varied songs.
Three, sometimes four, songs for every color.
I am countless.
I am the piano with an endless number of keys.
Sounds that no one has heard before.
A foreigner becomes familiar.
He feels tight at first like new boots,
Then suddenly he is like a second skin upon my feet.
The comfort of a friendship well worn.

I am the beggar. I am the thief.
Eight plus nine equals seventeen.
Is the exact answer to be questioned too?
In its garb of certainty
Is it camouflaged in this very certainty?
I am the illusion.
I am the veil and the mana behind the curtain.
I am a ripe fruit who bursts off of the tree.
Juicy and voluptuous.
Did someone design the taste we know as sweetness?
Or did it organically erupt into being?
Too delicious to stay out of existence.
I am the chicken, **and** I am the egg.
The seed and the bloom.
My one seed brings scores of new seeds into the world.
The sapling and the storm.
How else is the bark going to be tough enough for a long life?
The garbanzo bean boils in the pot so it may take up  flavor, Rumi tells.
No one ever said that the hot water didn't scald too.
Rub me with spices.
Lindseed oil, turpentine and Galkyd gel.
Brushes twirl in these chemicals then dip in my paint.
Cadmium red.
I live on cotton and linen canvases.
My hands feel more grace when they wield my cadmium red blood.
I live alone and weave pictures and words.
Poem is partner.
I live as wanderer.
I am never ending poetry
Cadmium red.
Swirl and twirl me upon your glass palette.
Prepare me for your chez d'oeuvre.
I am that morsel of truth that speaks upon cotton and linen canvases.
I was born as a tube of oil paint.
Serenade. Marmalade on warm toast with butter.
The perfect bite beholds a satisfying crunch and a taste that borders on wicked.
There is salt in the ocean,
So that we can really taste life,
and I bite into it like a fresh orange.
Life's juice spills down my pink chin.

I am the wolf on a journey to the moon.
The howl of sex.
I am bare skin.
With paint on my hands, I am the kneeding of flesh
Like fresh bread,
I cook with passion,
and I wear a crackling crust.
My fresh scent wafts throughout the *entire* house, not just the kitchen.
Fresh bread.
Mouth watering goodness.
With my belly full of bread,
I am the roundness of the pleasure of my satisfaction.
Sticky hands.
Coated in various honeys and maple syrups.
I am the splash of bourbon.
I am the glass bottle's pour.
A murder of ravens; a conspiracy of crows;
Black bodied birds within the air of sky.
The blue jay, the robin, the red cardinal
I am the woodpecker who pecks at tree bark; its hollow sounds;
I am the dream of sleep and the wildness of this poem that is the marrow of day.
I am cadmium red paint.

## Hallowed

My favorite word is hallowed.
Because to me, that word represents a stillness.
It is in the sacredness in between breath;
It is the ether
That moment right before the ballet
When the dancers can feel the potential energy
Of every momentum
That is about to course through their bodies
And their very souls.
Prayer hallows
And I am hollow within,
During its act,
Carved like stone by the light.
There lives the fierce war cry of my humanity.
And a delicious nothingness all at once.

## The Roar, the Attack

The warrior's run,
The attack of the sprint
My sharp tread slices the muddy ground.
Endorphins course in an accelerating pulse.
Spring blooms within my bleeding heart.
I raise my palms to my face as I cry.
I am comforted in my body's pelt.
I gasp, as I run so fast.
The warrior's run.
When those clouds clear and expose the truth that is the clean blue skies,
I am pierced by the beauty
Like the arrow's bullseye, straight in the heart

**Ripples in Water**

I drop my stone into the deep end of the water.
Mesmerized by the ripples that touch
Everyone and everything.
Your laugh was so powerful that
Even those in the darkest trenches of hell
Boots muddied and bloodied, fled the war.
Suddenly the senselessness of the monster was revealed
So they fled
Freed from the teeth of death.

I hear you cry
Your tears behold such a pure sorrow
That even across the farthest ocean
People and even the animals
Felt something profound stir within their hearts, within their ribcage.
Your grief likens to a ceremony
Sometimes the stone in the water just makes one *feel*.

For are we not all a part of a great tapestry?
Everyone a thread
Woven by choices and the winds of fates colliding,
A cosmic blanket that is stitched again and again everyday.

Just a thought over a cup of coffee and oat milk in a bustling cafe.

**The Hallows**
Hallowed chest
Like a white luminous tunnel of light
Sourced from my heart or perhaps something beyond
Upon witnessing something beautiful

**A Flower for Every Kiss**
I long to sing with you,
Before we kiss that is.
You stand behind me with your guitar,
And I am at the microphone
Singing, yes just singing.
Both of us feeling the rhythm of the song
Reverberating throughout our bones.
Then at the end lips graze lips
And there is a kiss.
There's the blooming of a flower for every kiss that has ever been.
You and I, we will have an entire meadow of flowers just for the kisses between us.
You and I will visit this meadow someday.
We will drink coffee and indulge in delectable treats while curled up on our quilted blanket.
I feed you strawberries.
Then I kiss your strawberry stained lips.
With the sun above me as my witness
We are to fall in love with each other
So bloom honey, yes bloom my heart with your tender kiss.

**Caught in My Butterfly Net**
Put the record on the player,
Let her spin, time after time,
Round after round.
Music for eternity.
My hips begin to sway
Your hands move my hair away from my neck.
Then your lips meet my bare skin.
The record holds the tempo for our kiss.
I am here.
So are you.
It's just another daydream caught in my butterfly net.

**A True Delight**

As I stare at the pistachio and filo dough dessert on my plate,

I notice that between its flaky layers,

It oozes with honey as I press upon its top with my metal fork.

Seemingly an endless quantity of amber nectar spills from its layers, sticky and sweet

And as I simply gaze at the sweet goo spill for a few moments,

I give a brief but profound prayer that my life may be like this little triangular treat.

May my life too ooze with its sweetness, always rich and satiating to live,

Oh so sweet my life is to be...

A treat to live with the fragrance of honey and pistachios. Life, a true delight.

**Fresh Life**
I sit by the fire.
And in its fierce red embers
I burn everything that I am ready to let go of;
All that does not serve me anymore.
Certain mistakes burn,
Past romances are given to the flame.
Wounds of mine burn away by the heat of the beast within the hearth.
Bit by bit, as pieces of my past burn,
Freshly I am awakened to the New.
Suddenly, there is so much room
To move around  in my new existence,
Now that the clutter has been turned to ash.
There is so much more air to breathe
And space to create.
I am a flood of flame
Burning the forest,
To make room for fresh life.

**Melted Heart**
As he steps into the room,
My heart melts the glass she's in.
Then she melts, herself.
Warm waxy heart flesh all over my sticky hands.
Because to the one who walked in the room, it's you that I want

**Blue Eyed Bird**
Blue eyed bird, oh blue eyed bird,
How you fly and soar in beauty.
Above the clouds,
Below the clouds
-and through
One with the skies.
You cry power,
And your power is one with your freedom.

## Bed

There she is...
I strip down into my undergarments,
I let my hair loose.
Then enter into my cave of blankets.
This coziness is as sweet as honey.
Upon landing on the soft mattress,
There is a sinking, then comes the spring
Romantic dreams with my head nestled perfectly on the cushioned pillow.
The bed is the perfect invention, oh yes it is.

**Words that Thaw**

The blooming of a flower
One winter's coming and the thaw that takes her away.
The length of a love song.
The steam from a kiss in the cold.
Hot pancakes cooking on the griddle.
Small sticky fingers
Grabbing to satiate.
Full bellies.
The warmth of the butterfly's cocoon,
Only to emerge into free air.
Set free into their new cocoon of sky.
The lark's call, a cry of wildness.
Before she dives into the lake.
It haunts, with its similarity to a woman's voice.

**Those with Golden Hearts**

I live cradled like a babe.
I am nursed by tea leaves and hot water.
The ones with golden hearts help me be better than I think I might be.
To fully occupy my life.
Words that shine through with golden auras,
Like service and altruism.
Words that feel good to say
And even better to emulate.

## Ahimsa

On my knees in the grass,
I light a candle,
Green light, sun and
fresh spring leaves
Every candle a prayer for ahimsa.
No harm.

**Choice**
With open palms
I face myself in the mirror
A meandering choice
Right or left
Earth or sky.

# THE END

Made in the USA
Monee, IL
09 August 2023

40698174R00090